AF351308

This book
belongs to:

____

____

____

____

Dear CHEETAH® family:

Our little books were specially created to help our early readers master their decoding skills and build reading fluency. The repetitive use of high-frequency words, word families, decodable words, rhymes, and vivid illustrations facilitates this process. Our stories complement the objectives and content highlighted in the Jamaica Early Childhood Curriculum Guide and the Ministry of Education and Youth Grade I National Standards Curriculum.

In journeying through our series, our little ones will develop a deeper awareness of, and appreciation for, our Jamaican culture. Our books also have universal appeal, as any early reader can identify with the characters, events and subjects in our texts. Readers will get to enjoy the stories, build vocabulary, and exercise critical thinking by engaging in the activities at the end of each story.

Additionally, as a precursor to our series, or as a support to it, we've created a decodable 'sentence strip' book for the very young readers and those who require more scaffolding.

Happy reading!

CHEETAH®

Chasing and capturing your dreams with you.

Just like a scientist uses a telescope to explore the stars, readers use letters to explore the universe of stories. Let's go! Let's explore the universe of stories!

My decodable words:

dew, few, new, stew, hot, not, pot

Letter sounds:

- long vowel sound /ū/ as in digraphs 'ew', 'ui' and 'ue' in the final position in words.

Word families: 'ew', 'ot'

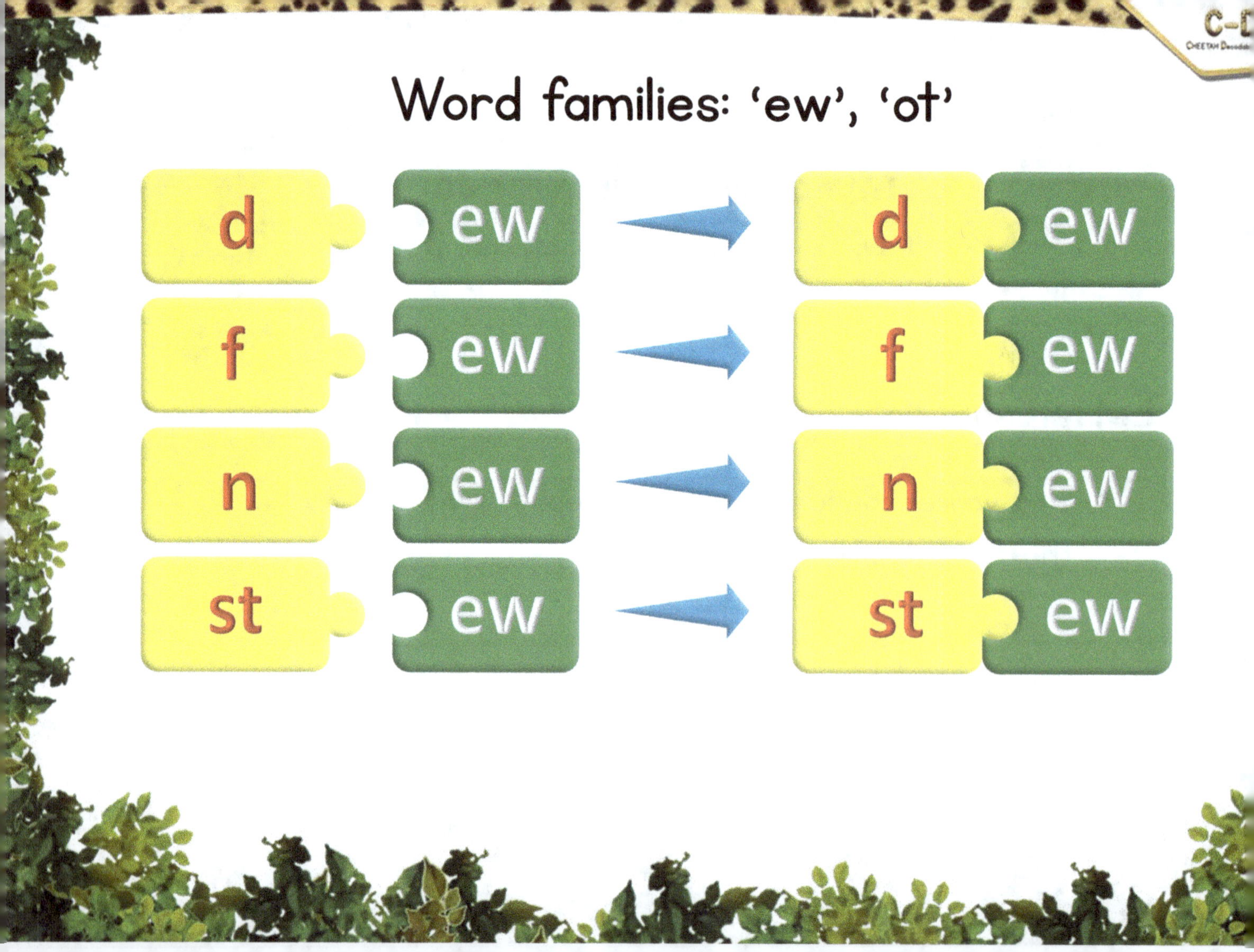

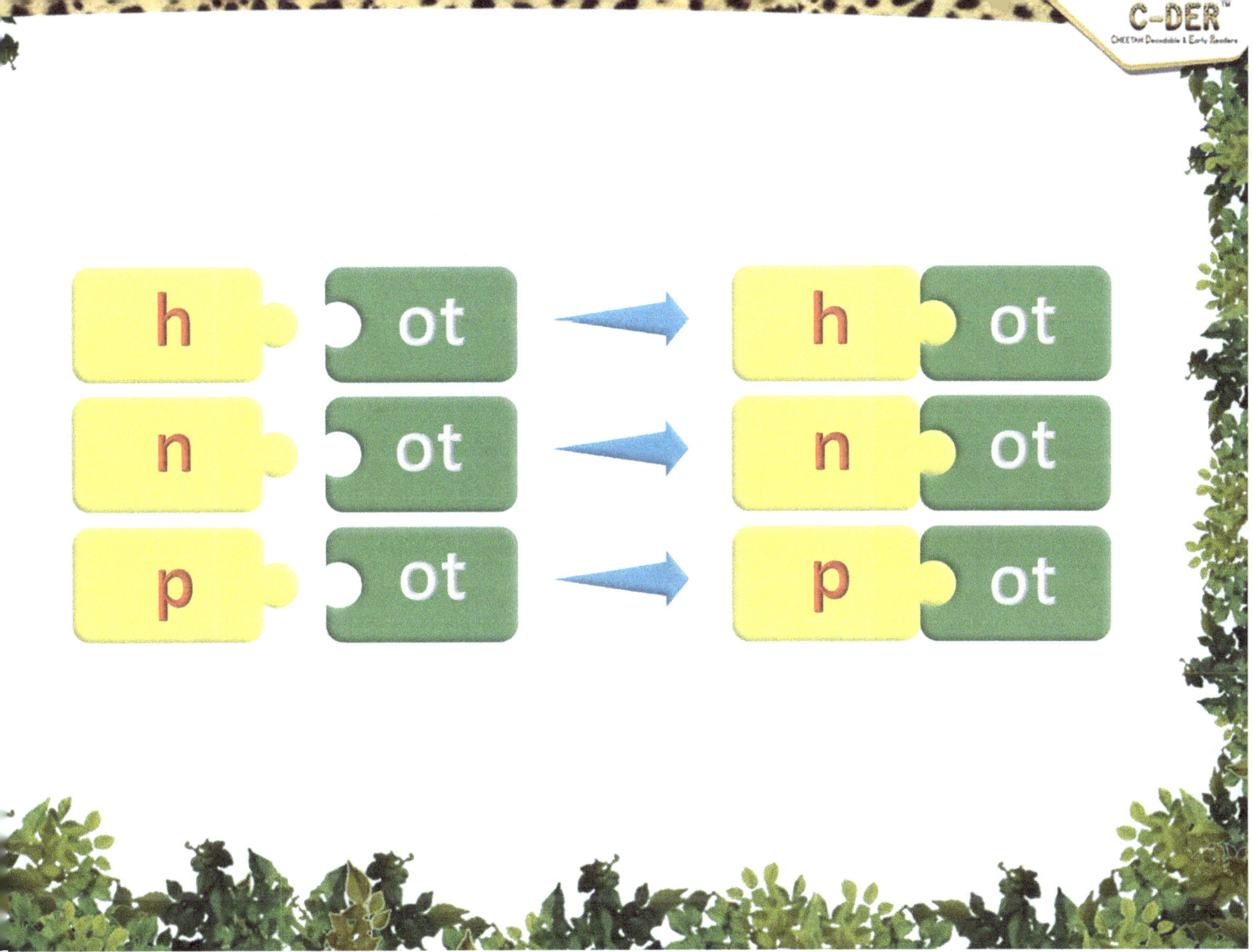

h
ot
h ot
n
ot
n ot
p
ot
p ot
C-DER

C-DER
CHEETAH Decodable & Early Readers
1

What's Cooking?

We get up early; there is lots to do.

It is a special day. Mom is making stew.

Ben brings in some fruits still wet with dew,

and he takes them to the kitchen for Aunt Sue.

3

Mom cooks the beef stew in a big pot.
Soon, the pot is very, very hot.
Aunt Sue cuts the fruits to make
banana cake,

then she puts it into the oven to bake.

Aunt Sue always helps mom on special days.

I love it when she comes over and stays.

They always make new things to eat.

When Aunt Sue comes over, we are in for a treat!

7

Mom and Aunt Sue go out
of the kitchen.

They go to the other rooms
and start cleaning.

I stay in the kitchen to
check on the food.

Ooh! I love the smell! The
food smells so good!

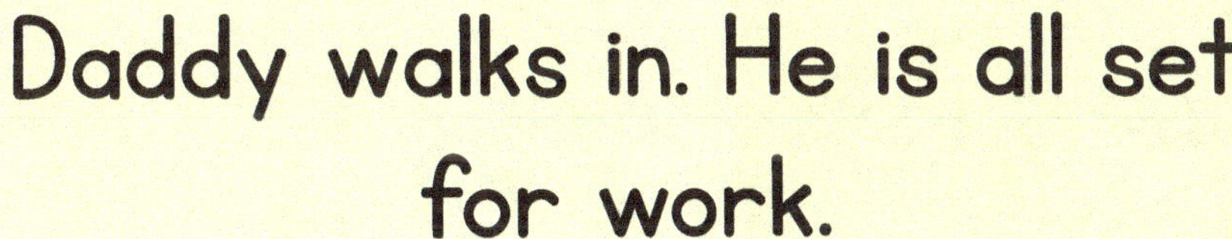

Daddy walks in. He is all set for work.

He works in town as a bank clerk.

He sits to eat before he goes...

and the smell of the stew goes up to his nose.

11

'Hmmm…I must see what is inside that pot.

I think I will take a peek, why not!

I want to see what smells so good.

I cannot wait to eat that food.'

13

He takes a spoon, then goes to the pot.

He lifts the lid... 'Oh my! It is hot!'

The steam is so hot that it burns his nose.

SPLASH! He drops the spoon in, and stew gets on his clothes!

'Oh no!' Dad says, 'what am I going to do? Now I will be late because of this stew!'

Mom walks in and says, 'Well, here is a lesson for you:

Never, ever mess with a hot pot of stew!'

Discussion and activities:

1. Have the children share their experiences of instances when they got into an incident which involved their clothes getting soiled. Have them talk about how they dealt with the situation.

2. Have the children identify the words with the target letters and sound.

3. Have the children make the sound of the target letters and identify rhyming words in the text.

Discussion and activities:

4. Discuss the words: dew, steam, peek and stew as used in the context of the story.

5. Have the children read the text aloud.

Questions:

1. What special occasion do you think they were preparing for in the story?

   ....

2. How do you think Dad could have prevented the incident in the story?

   ....

What do cheetahs eat for dessert? Zebra cake!

www.ingramcontent.com/pod-product-compliance
Lightning Source LLC
Chambersburg PA
CBHW082041150726
47996CB00016B/3259